THE DECLARATION OF INDEPENDENCE

in Translation
What It Really Means

Revised Edition

by Amie Jane Leavitt

Consultant:
Dana Stefanelli, PhD candidate
Corcoran Department of History
University of Virginia, Charlottesville

CAPSTONE PRESS
a capstone imprint

Fact Finders is published by Capstone Press,
1710 Roe Crest Drive, North Mankato, Minnesota 56003.
www.mycapstone.com

Library of Congress Cataloging-in-Publication Data is available on the Library of Congress Website

ISBN: 978-1-5157-9137-9 (revised hardcover)
ISBN: 978-1-5157-6250-8 (revised paperback)
ISBN: 978-1-5157-6247-8 (ebook pdf)

Editorial Credits
Megan Schoeneberger, editor; Gene Bentdahl, set designer and illustrator; Wanda Winch, photo researcher

Photo Credits
Bridgeman Images: Ken Welsh/Private Collection, 18-19
Capstone Studio: Karon Dubke, Cover Bottom, 7 Top, 11 Bottom Right, 21, 28
EyeWire: Photodisc, 9
Getty Images Inc: The Image Bank/Jurgen Vogt, 26
iStockphoto: Pictore, 25
National Archives and Records Administration (NARA): Charters of Freedom, 4 Right, 5, 6 Right
National Guard Image Gallery: "The Shot Heard 'Round the World" by Domenick D'Andrea, 17
North Wind Picture Archives: 4 Left, 8, 22
Shutterstock: Burlingham, 11 Left, Everett – Art, 13, Susan Law Cain, 20
SuperStock, Inc: 6 Left, 15 Right, Huntington Library, 14
The New York Public Library: Manuscripts and Archives Division, 15 Left
Thinkstock: Photos.com, 10, 23
Wikimedia: White House Historical Association, Cover top, 7 Bottom

Note: Essential content terms are bold and are defined at the bottom of the page where they first appear.

Table of Contents

CHAPTER 1

The Declaration of Independence

A HISTORIC DAY IN PHILADELPHIA

July 4, 1776, started out like an ordinary day in Philadelphia. Yet something remarkable was happening inside the State House. The Second Continental Congress was making one of the most important decisions in American history.

Two days earlier, Congress had voted for independence. Now the delegates were taking another look at Thomas Jefferson's **Declaration** of Independence. The men agreed that it explained exactly why the colonies needed to break free from Great Britain and its ruler, King George III.

declaration — announcement

The Congress asked local printer John Dunlap to print about 200 copies of the declaration. Congress sent copies to all of the colonies and to the Continental army's commanding officers.

Dunlap printed the declaration in his newspaper, the *Pennsylvania Evening Post*, on July 6, 1776. On July 8, the document was read aloud in Philadelphia's town square. And on July 9, George Washington read it to his troops.

After the Declaration of Independence was read, many patriots cheered with excitement. In some places, the colonists even celebrated with fireworks.

But the men who signed the declaration had little time to celebrate. They had spoken against Great Britain. With their pens, they risked their lives for freedom.

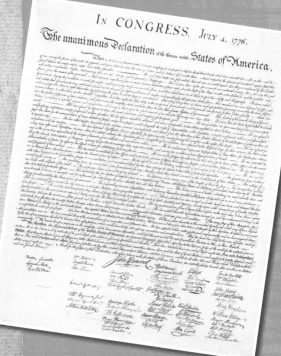

So what exactly does the declaration say, and what do its words mean to you? Turn the page to find out.

CHAPTER 2

The Declaration of Independence

A DOCUMENT THAT CHANGED THE WORLD

The Declaration of Independence

In Congress, July 4, 1776.

The **unanimous** Declaration of the thirteen united States of America,

When in the Course of human events, it becomes necessary for one people to **dissolve** the political bands which have connected them with another, and to assume among the powers of the earth, the separate and equal station to which the Laws of Nature and of Nature's God entitle them, a decent respect to the opinions of mankind requires that they should declare the causes which impel them to the separation.

dissolve — break up

unanimous — in complete agreement

Before the Declaration of Independence, Great Britain ruled the 13 colonies.

What?

The 13 colonies in America have agreed as one to break ties with **Great Britain**. Both nature and God have given people this right. Now the people will tell **the world** why.

Congress wanted other countries to support their cause. Later, France helped the United States fight for independence.

Huh?

Thomas Jefferson, the main author of the Declaration of Independence, loved words. He especially loved big words. We don't have room to define them all. But if you're curious, grab your dictionary.

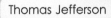

Thomas Jefferson

The Declaration of Independence Continued

We hold these truths to be self-evident, that all men are created equal, that they are endowed by their Creator with certain **unalienable** Rights, that among these are Life, Liberty and the pursuit of Happiness.

Equality for All?

The Declaration of Independence says that everybody is created equal. But in 1776, equality applied only to some people. At that time, millions of Africans in the 13 colonies were slaves. Women could not vote or own property. American Indians were forced off their native lands. It wasn't a perfect world in 1776. But with the declaration, Congress set into motion a form of government that in time would include all people. The nation still isn't perfect, but it's a lot better than it was back then.

unalienable — can't be taken away

Some rights should be clear to everyone. For one thing, all **men** are equal. God gave people certain rights that nobody can take away. These rights include the right to life and a right to freedom. People should be free to **find happiness**.

The declaration doesn't say that we have a right to be happy. It says we have the right to try to be happy. Happiness is a goal, not a promise.

Today we would say "people" instead of "men."

The Declaration of Independence Continued

That to secure these rights, Governments are instituted among Men, deriving their just powers from the consent of the governed, — That whenever any Form of Government becomes destructive to these ends, it is the Right of the People to alter or to **abolish** it, and to institute new Government, laying its foundation on such principles and organizing its powers in such form, as to them shall seem most likely to effect their Safety and Happiness. Prudence, indeed, will dictate that Governments long established should not be changed for light and transient causes;

Mobs of colonists tried to force British officials to resign.

abolish — put an end to

What?

Governments should protect the rights of their people. Governments get their powers from the people they serve. If a government fails to **protect** its citizens, then the citizens should change the government. Citizens should do this for really good reasons, not for silly ones.

One way that governments protect people is through fair laws.

Today U.S. citizens can change the government by voting. But the colonists didn't have that right.

11

The Declaration of Independence Continued

and accordingly all experience hath shewn, that mankind are more disposed to suffer, while evils are sufferable, than to right themselves by abolishing the forms to which they are accustomed. But when a long train of abuses and usurpations, pursuing invariably the same Object evinces a design to reduce them under absolute Despotism, it is their right, it is their duty, to throw off such Government, and to provide new Guards for their future security. — Such has been the patient sufferance of these Colonies; and such is now the necessity which constrains them to alter their former Systems of Government. The history of the present King of Great Britain is a history of repeated injuries and usurpations, all having in direct object the establishment of an absolute **Tyranny** over these States. To prove this, let Facts be submitted to a candid world . . . .

tyranny — a cruel or unfair government

What?

People often choose to suffer instead of making changes. Colonists have <u>tried to be patient</u>, but their suffering must end. Enough is enough. The colonies have the responsibility to end Great Britain's unfair control. King George III has a history of cruelty. He is a tyrant. Let the world know what he has done wrong.

The colonists asked the king for fair treatment. He never listened. He acted like their opinions didn't matter.

King George III

The Top Five Complaints

At this point, Jefferson and the colonists included a long list of complaints about King George III. Instead of the whole list, here are the main points.

5. He fired leaders who didn't agree with him or do what he said.
4. He didn't punish British soldiers for hurting or even killing the colonists.
3. He made the colonists give food and shelter to British soldiers.
2. He forced the colonists to join his navy.
1. He didn't give colonists any say in making laws.

The Declaration of Independence Continued

. . . In every stage of these Oppressions We have **Petitioned** for **Redress** in the most humble terms: Our repeated Petitions have been answered only by repeated injury. A Prince whose character is thus marked by every act which may define a Tyrant, is unfit to be the ruler of a free people.

Benjamin Franklin (standing at left) went to Great Britain to plead for fair treatment of the colonies.

petition — ask

redress — correcting something that is wrong or unfair

What?

Through all this poor treatment, we tried to work with the king. We sent <u>letters</u> to the king, asking him to respect our rights. He ignored us. Instead, he just made things worse. The king is a <u>cruel leader</u>. He is not worthy of ruling the colonies.

In this letter, colonists tried to gain more rights from Great Britain.

The colonists called the king a tyrant. A tyrant is a leader who uses his power harshly.

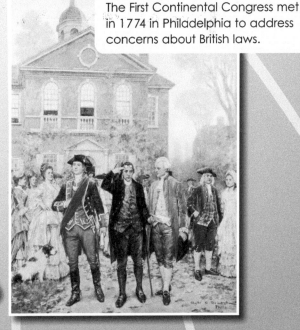

The First Continental Congress met in 1774 in Philadelphia to address concerns about British laws.

The Declaration of Independence Continued

Nor have We been wanting in attentions to our British brethren. We have warned them from time to time of attempts by their legislature to extend an unwarrantable jurisdiction over us. We have reminded them of the circumstances of our emigration and settlement here. We have appealed to their native justice and magnanimity, and we have conjured them by the ties of our common kindred to disavow these usurpations, which, would inevitably interrupt our connections and correspondence. They too have been deaf to the voice of justice and of consanguinity. We must, therefore, acquiesce in the necessity, which denounces our Separation, and hold them, as we hold the rest of mankind, Enemies in War, in Peace Friends.

What?

We didn't go to just the king about these problems. We also tried to talk to the British people and their lawmakers. We reminded them why we left Europe and came to America. Many of us **came from Great Britain**. We asked for their help because we were brothers. But they would not listen either. So now we must separate ourselves from all of Great Britain. We are now **enemies at war**. When the war ends, we will be friends again.

When the Declaration of Independence was written, the Revolutionary War had already been going on for nearly 15 months. The first shots of the war were fired at Lexington and Concord in Massachusetts on April 19, 1775.

Many of the colonists considered themselves British. It was difficult to cut ties with their homeland.

The Declaration of Independence Continued

We, therefore, the Representatives of the united States of America, in General Congress, Assembled, appealing to the Supreme Judge of the world for the rectitude of our intentions, do, in the Name, and by the Authority of the good People of these Colonies, solemnly publish and declare, That these United Colonies are, and of Right ought to be Free and Independent States; that they are **Absolved** from all **Allegiance** to the British Crown, and that all political connection between them and the state of Great Britain, is and ought to be totally dissolved;

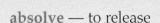

absolve — to release

allegiance — duty and loyalty

As **representatives** of the American people, we declare these colonies to be free states. The king is no longer our ruler. We break all ties with Great Britain.

Every colony sent a delegate to the Second Continental Congress. These delegates tried to vote as the people in their colonies would have voted.

members of the Second Continental Congress

The Declaration of Independence Continued

and that as Free and Independent States, they have full Power to levy War, conclude Peace, contract Alliances, establish Commerce, and to do all other Acts and Things which Independent States may of right do. And for the support of this Declaration, with a firm reliance on the protection of divine Providence, we mutually **pledge** to each other our Lives, our Fortunes and our sacred Honor.

John Hancock's Signature

John Hancock's signature is the largest on the document. Legend has it that Hancock wanted the king to be able to read it without his glasses. This story is untrue. His signature is in the center and is the largest for two reasons. First, he was the president of the Continental Congress. Second, he always signed his name like this.

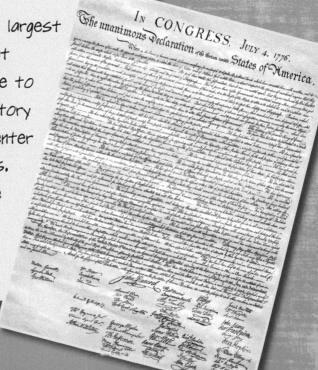

pledge — promise

As free states, we have the same powers as other countries. We can go to war, make agreements, and trade with other countries. We believe God will help protect us. **We now sign** our names to this declaration. By signing, we are putting our lives, our money and property, and our reputations **on the line**.

The Declaration of Independence was actually signed by most of the delegates in August.

If the colonies lost the war, the signers could lose everything — including their lives.

CHAPTER 3

The Declaration of Independence

WHY INDEPENDENCE?

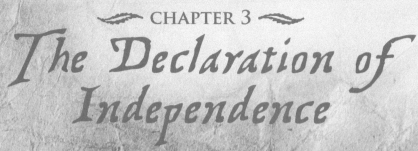

The colonists' problems with the British began after the French and Indian War (1754–1763). The British spent a lot of money on this war for control of North America. Now, the British felt the colonists should pay that money back. King George III raised taxes on everything from sugar and tea to paper goods and clothing.

the French and Indian War

No Say in the Government

The colonists didn't think this was fair. All of these new laws were made in Great Britain. The colonists didn't have a say. The colonists wanted to make the laws that affected them.

But the king wouldn't listen. He didn't care what the colonists thought. Soon, some colonists rebelled. Some threw barrels of tea into Boston Harbor. This event became known as the Boston Tea Party.

Finally, in 1774, a group of colonial leaders met in Philadelphia. During the First Continental Congress, leaders talked about the problems in the colonies. They sent a letter to the king asking to be heard. Little was done to make things right.

Boston Tea Party

The Revolutionary War

The next April, things grew worse in Massachusetts. The king ordered his army to take away the colonists' weapons. The colonists fought back. The battles of Lexington and Concord were the first battles of the Revolutionary War.

Road to Independence

Some colonists started talking about independence. This was a dangerous thing to do. Talking about revolting against your government is **treason**. This crime can be punished by death.

In January 1776, Thomas Paine printed a pamphlet called *Common Sense*. In it, he wrote about the idea of independence. Many colonists read his pamphlet and agreed with Paine's ideas.

On June 7, 1776, Virginia delegate Richard Henry Lee spoke at the Continental Congress. He talked about independence. This was the first time the delegates ever discussed this idea.

treason — the crime of being disloyal to your country

The men argued about independence for two long days. Finally, many of the delegates agreed with what Lee said. They had tried to make peace with the king. Now they had only one option left.

A few weeks later, five men were asked to write a document describing why the colonies should become independent. This committee of five included Thomas Jefferson, Benjamin Franklin, John Adams, Robert Livingston, and Roger Sherman. The document they wrote, the Declaration of Independence, was accepted by Congress on July 4, 1776.

The Document

The original copy of the document still exists more than 200 years after it was written. You can see it in the National Archives in Washington, D.C. It is part of an exhibit called the Charters of Freedom. The Declaration of Independence sits next to the original copies of the U.S. Constitution and the Bill of Rights.

the committee of five

A Living Legacy

The Declaration of Independence was not just important in 1776. It has continued to be important for more than 200 years. During the Civil War, President Abraham Lincoln used some of the ideas from the declaration in his speeches. When women tried to get the same rights as men, they turned to the declaration too.

Even today, many people around the world still hope to form a government that will protect their "life, liberty, and pursuit of happiness."

the Declaration of Independence on display at the National Archives

Great Britain and France fight the French and Indian War.

1754–1763

Colonists dump tea into Boston Harbor in what becomes known as the Boston Tea Party.

December 1773

The first shots of the Revolutionary War are fired at Lexington and Concord in Massachusetts.

April 19, 1775

The Second Continental Congress meets in Philadelphia. John Hancock is elected its president.

May 1775

Thomas Jefferson and the committee of five present the Declaration of Independence to Congress.

June 28, 1776

Congress votes to accept the Declaration of Independence.

July 4, 1776

President Abraham Lincoln refers to the Declaration of Independence in his Gettysburg Address.

November 19, 1863

Why Do I Care?

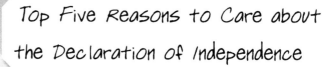

Top Five Reasons to Care about the Declaration of Independence

5. The Declaration of Independence is why Americans celebrate Independence Day on July 4 every year.

4. If the colonists hadn't risked everything to make this declaration, Americans might still have a king and queen.

3. The Declaration of Independence inspired other nations to seek independence.

2. The Declaration of Independence gave a new purpose to the soldiers fighting the Revolutionary War.

1. The Declaration of Independence helped establish the freedoms that Americans enjoy today.

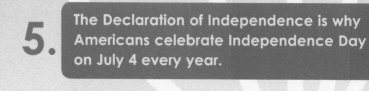

Translation Guide

consanguinity — This isn't an Italian pasta dish. It's a relationship or connection.

hath — Did Thomas Jefferson have a lisp? No! "Hath" is a fancy way of saying "has" or "have."

rectitude — This kind of sounds like something you might say if you crashed your bike — "I wrecked it, dude!" But this word actually refers to correctness or goodness.

redress — No, we're not talking about putting your clothes on again. Redress means to make something right or to correct something that is unfair or wrong.

unalienable — This word has nothing to do with space aliens. It actually means that something can't be given or taken away.

usurpation — Do "you-surp" your soda with a straw? No, usurpation is taking something away from someone else, usually in an unfair way.

Glossary

abolish (uh-BOL-ish) — to put an end to something officially

absolve (ab-ZOLV) — to pardon something or free the person from blame

allegiance (uh-LEE-junss) — loyal support for someone or something

declaration (dek-luh-RAY-shuhn) — the act of announcing something, or the announcement made

dissolve (di-ZOLV) — to officially end

petition (puh-TISH-uhn) — to make a formal request

pledge (PLEJ) — to make a sincere promise

redress (ree-DRESS) — a solution or correction

treason (TREE-zuhn) — the crime of being disloyal to your country or government

tyranny (TIHR-uh-nee) — a cruel or unfair government in which all power is in the hands of a single ruler

unalienable (uhn-AY-lee-uhn-uh-buhl) — impossible to take away

unanimous (yoo-NAN-uh-muhss) — agreed on by everyone

Use FactHound to find Internet sites related to this book.

Visit **www.facthound.com**

Just type in **9781515791379** and go.

Coddington, Andrew. *Thomas Jefferson: Architect of the Declaration of Independence.* Buffalo, New York: Cavendish Square, 2017.

Manger, Katherine. *The Declaration of Independence.* New York: Rosen Publishing, 2017.

Raum, Elizabeth. *The Declaration of Independence.* Documenting U.S. History. Mankato, Minn.: Capstone, 2013.

Index